Wales Coast Path: Pembrokeshire South

CW01023943

Text: Dennis Kelsall

Series editor: Tony Bowerman

Photographs: Dennis Kelsall, The National Library of Wales, © Crown copyright (2015) Visit Wales, Pembrokeshire Coastal Photography/ www.pemcoastphotos.com, Drew Buckley/ www. drewbuckleyphotography.com, Vivienne Crow, Tony Bowerman, Dreamstime, Shutterstock

Design: Carl Rogers

Northern Eye Books

ISBN 978-1-908632-30-2

A CIP catalogue record for this book is available from the British Library.

Cover: 'Green Bridge of Wales' near Castlemartin (Walk 5)

Important Advice: The routes described in this book are undertaken at the reader's own risk. Walkers should take into account their level of fitness, wear suitable footwear and clothing, and carry food and water. It is also advisable to take the relevant OS map with you in case you get lost and leave the area covered by our maps.

Whilst every care has been taken to ensure the accuracy of the route directions, the publishers cannot accept responsibility for errors or omissions, or for changes in the details given. Nor can the publisher and copyright owners accept responsibility for any consequences arising from the use of this book.

If you find any inaccuracies in either the text or maps, please either write to us or email us at the addresses below. Thank you.

First published in 2015 by:

Northern Eye Books Limited
Northern Eye Books, Tattenhall, Cheshire CH3 9PX
Reprinted 2016, 2019

Email: tony@northerneyebooks.com

For sales enquiries, please call 01928 723 744

www.walescoastpath.co.uk
www.northerneyebooks.co.uk

 Instagram: @wales_coast_path

 Twitter: @WalesCoastUK
@Northerneyeboo

Contents

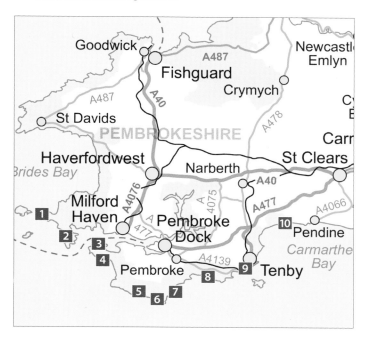

Britain's Only Coastal National Park

Although several of Britain's National Parks have a seaward boundary, only the Pembrokeshire park was specifically created to protect the coast. Facing the Atlantic, its coastline runs for 200 miles around the westernmost tip of Wales. The Pembrokeshire coast is a place of haunting beauty and perpetual contrast.

In places, a wild and untamed landscape faces the full fury of ocean storms, while elsewhere, craggy-cliffed headlands and fractured promontories protect coves and deep inlets backed by lush woodland. The rocks from which it is formed span more than 700 million years and few places in Britain possess such a concentration of dramatic geological features. Nature and a rich human heritage come together in a backdrop of stunning and ever-changing scenery, in which a profusion of wildflowers, birds and wildlife exploits the diversity of natural habitats.

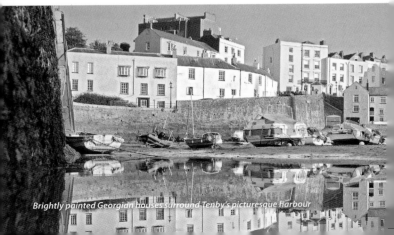

Brightly painted Georgian houses surround Tenby's picturesque harbour

South Pembrokeshire Coast

The Pembrokeshire coast alters subtly from north to south.
The southern rocks are far younger and the coast tends to be
south-facing, creating a gentler hinterland. This influenced
historical development and culture, for although the Norman
advance extended throughout Pembrokeshire, settlement
focused on the more fertile southern corner. It became known
as 'Little England', with English rather than Welsh spoken, a
tradition reflected in place names. Before reliable roads, trade
and prosperity favoured the coast, and because the railways
came late here, Pembrokeshire was largely ignored by the
Industrial Revolution. Unspoiled and breathtakingly scenic,
the coast is captivating every step of the way.

> "… in all the broad lands of Wales, Manorbier is
> the most pleasant place by far."

Giraldus Cambrensis, 1188

TOP 10 Walks: Pembrokeshire South

WHILE ALMOST EVERY SCRAP OF THE SOUTH PEMBROKESHIRE COAST is worthy of inclusion, the ten walks described in this book have been carefully chosen to reveal its ever-changing character — from popular bays and beaches and seaside resorts to wild and rugged cliffs where soaring seabirds might be your only company. All are circular, but you might take advantage of the excellent buses that service all the main access points along the Pembrokeshire stretch of the Wales Coast Path. It's superb coastal walking.

The Marloes peninsula page 8

The Dale peninsula page 14

The Angle peninsula page 20

Freshwater West & Angle page 24

Looking across Jack Sound to Skomer from Deer Park, on the Marloes peninsula

The **Marloes peninsula**

An easy circuit of the tip of South Pembrokeshire's most island-strewn promontory, linking two of its finest strands

What to expect:
Rugged clifftop paths with occasional ups and downs, a short crossland section on lanes

Distance/time: 11.5km/ 7¼ miles. Allow 3 to 3½ hours

Start: National Trust car park (charge) off lane west of Marloes

Grid ref: SM 778 082

Ordnance Survey Map: OS Explorer OL36 (South Pembrokeshire)

After the walk: The Lobster Pot Inn, Marloes SA62 3AZ | 01646 636233, OR Clock House café, Marloes SA62 3AZ | 01646 636527

Walk outline

The route follows a track to Marloes Sands, joining the Wales Coast Path above the beach. Heading west, the cliffs become increasingly rugged, offering views to the islands and perhaps glimpses of seals in the rocky coves below. Around Wooltack Point and beyond Martin's Haven, the walk returns along a gentler northern coast, turning back inland above Musselwick Sands to finish along a quiet lane.

The Marloes peninsula

A slender fingertip disintegrating to a string of offshore islands and pointing to the Atlantic beyond, the Marloes peninsula forms the southern-most cusp of St Bride's Bay.

Marloes is a place of both great beauty and natural significance and most of the peninsula is managed by the National Trust. At its heart is Marloes Mere, a grazing marsh that attracts winter waders, wildfowl and birds of prey. The sound between Wooltack Point and Skomer is an important marine nature reserve, while the three main islands are bird reserves. Boats leave Martin's Haven for Skomer.

Boat to Skomer

Skomer puffin

The Walk

1. Leave the southern end of the car park's track and follow the lane left. After 100 metres, turn off on a track through a gate on the right, which leads down to **Marloes Sands**.

2. Just before reaching the beach, watch for the **Wales Coast Path** leaving on the right. The way undulates high above sawtoothed rocks that back the strand. Past the far end of the beach the path curves above a point overlooking Gateholm Island.

3. Beyond, the view looks down on **Albion Sands**, where at low water, two pipes protruding from the sand are all that remain of a wreck.

The beach takes its name from the paddle steamer Albion, which came to grief off the coast, just six years after its launch in 1831. Carrying passengers and a cargo of strong drink, pigs and horses from Cork to Bristol, it had sailed through Jack Sound, but then in swerving to avoid a small boat, struck a rock and was holed off Midland Isle. The captain managed to beach the ship on the sands in the lee of Gateholm Island, enabling the crew and passengers to clamber safely ashore.

Carry on above the inhospitable coast, where shattered rocks deny any hope of safe landing. Approaching the peninsula, pass through a gate and cross

Broken coast: *The long nose of Wooltack Point marks the southern end of St Brides Bay*

a plank bridge. The path left swings above a small sandy cove, **Renny Slip** to the boundary wall of the **Deer Park**.

4. Stick with the cliff path to the far extremity of **Wooltack Point,** which overlooks Jack Sound and Midland Isle to Skomer.

Wooltack Point, Skomer, Grassholm and the distant Smalls are all part of the same geological formation, outcrops of a belt of hard volcanic rock that extends along the northern side of the peninsula. Skokholm and Gateholm, however, are completely different and composed of Old Red Sandstone, which appears again in Walk 2 on St Ann's Head. The isolation of the islands attracts breeding sea birds; Skomer and Skokholm have the world's largest population of Manx shearwaters, while the gannets on Grassholm are so numerous that they can be seen from the mainland as a cloud above the island.

Heading back, branch left to a white **lookout post** on the highpoint of the headland.

Deep blue sea: *Skomer from the cliff path between Deer Park and Marloes*

The small hut overlooking the Deer Park commands a view 18 miles out to sea. It was originally a Coastguard lookout, but is now manned by volunteers of the National Coastwatch Institution.

Beyond, the path falls across an Iron Age wall to a gate in the 'modern' wall and out onto the corner of a track.

5. You can follow the lane ahead up to the **Lockwood Centre**, where there's local wildlife information and a small shop. Otherwise, go left, passing **toilets** and an **information centre** explaining the marine nature reserve. Just after the toilets, look in the wall for an **ancient stone**, faintly inscribed with a ringed cross.

Just before **Martin's Haven** beach, turn off right with the Coast Path, climbing steps onto the low cliffs. Although not as dramatic as the southern coast, it remains a fine walk, with distant views across St Brides Bay to the St David's peninsula and Ramsey Island (see *Top Ten Walks – Pembrokeshire North*). Carry on for 3 kilometres to a junction of paths above **Musselwick Sands**.

6. Ahead, the Coast Path drops steeply and offers access to the superb beach

below. The way back, however, lies to the right, turning in beside a narrow gully and signed to 'Marloes'. Towards the top of the gully, the path swings right and continues beside a field to reach a lane.

7. Go right and walk for 800 metres to a junction. Turn left beside a house and follow the narrow lane back to the car park to complete the walk. ♦

Deer Park
Part of the Kensington estate centred on St Brides Castle, the Deer Park was enclosed during the 19th century, but never held any deer. The far older stone rubble bank behind the enclosure wall is an Iron Age boundary that protected a large settlement on the headland. There were prehistoric settlements on Gateholm and Skomer too. In fact, the Iron Age hut circles, field boundaries and cairns on Skomer are some of the most complete in Europe.

St Ann's Head lighthouse guides ships past rocks at the entrance to Milford Haven

The **Dale peninsula**

A fine circular walk around the perimeter of the Dale peninsula — said to be the sunniest spot in all Wales

What to expect:
Good clifftop and field edge paths. Quiet lanes at the start. Several ups and downs

Distance/time: 11km/ 7 miles. Allow 3 to 3½ hours

Start: Public car park (pay and display) at Dale

Grid ref: SM 810 058

Ordnance Survey Map: OS Explorer OL36 (South Pembrokeshire)

After the walk: Griffin Inn, Dale SA62 3RB | 01646 636227, OR Boat House Café, Dale SA62 3RB | 01646 636642

Walk outline
Beginning along the seafront, the route follows a wooded lane towards Dale Point. Crossing the neck, it rejoins the coast past a succession of sandy bays to the lighthouse station on St Ann's Head. The return up the western side of the headland runs along rugged cliffs before dropping to the sandy beach of Westdale Bay. A short tramp across fields and along a quiet lane returns you to Dale.

The Dale peninsula
The Dale peninsula, along with that at Angle, overlooks the entrance to Milford Haven, one of the finest deepwater harbours in the world.

During the 19th century, when there was a real threat of Napoleonic invasion, it became one of the most heavily defended places in the country to protect the naval shipyard at Pembroke Dock. Although now adapted to other uses, the military buildings on Dale Point and West Blockhouse Point can still be seen. More recent are the navigation markers that help pilot shipping through this busy, narrow channel. Passed too are the lighthouses on St Ann's Head, welcome beacons that have long guided navigators along this treacherous coast.

Navigation markers

Porpoise

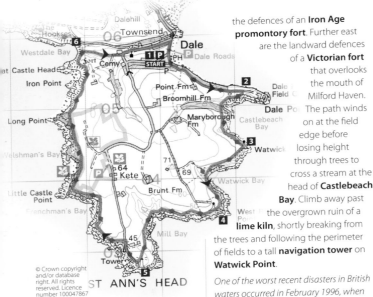

0   1km
              1 mile

the defences of an **Iron Age promontory fort**. Further east are the landward defences of a **Victorian fort** that overlooks the mouth of Milford Haven. The path winds on at the field edge before losing height through trees to cross a stream at the head of **Castlebeach Bay**. Climb away past the overgrown ruin of a **lime kiln**, shortly breaking from the trees and following the perimeter of fields to a tall **navigation tower** on **Watwick Point**.

One of the worst recent disasters in British waters occurred in February 1996, when the bulk tanker MV Sea Empress *struck rocks in the channel while attempting to enter Milford Haven. More than half its 130,000 ton cargo of oil leaked onto the sea causing unprecedented pollution in one of the country's most important marine nature reserves. Thousands of seabirds were killed and oil on the beaches decimated seaweeds, shellfish and invertebrates. The cleanup took more than a year.*

The Walk

1. Turn right from the car park and follow the shore road into **Dale**. Keep left at successive junctions behind the **harbour** to climb away along a leafy lane. After a kilometre, having left the woods behind and nearing the **Dale Fort Field Centre**, watch for the **Wales Coast Path** leaving through a gate on the right.

2. Walk away beside the bank of a ditch,

3. Keep going above the coast. Towards the far corner of the third field, the path

Victorian gun battery: *Built in the 1890s, Dale Fort is now run as a Field Studies centre*

leaves left to wind above the head of **Watwick Bay**. At a fork, the left branch drops steeply to the beach, an idyllic spot more than amply justifying the climb back. The ongoing path continues to **West Blockhouse Point** where, as its name suggests, there is a **Victorian blockhouse** as well as three more **navigation markers**.

4. Skirt them on the landward side and then pass gun emplacements on the right. The way falls to **Mill Bay**,

crossing a couple of streams at its head. Climb away and continue at the field edge, watching for a **stone marker** commemorating Henry Tudor's landing from France in 1485. Approaching the settlement on **St Ann's Head**, leave the field through a gate and follow a path past walled gardens that once fed the small community, continuing beyond the corner toward the **lighthouse**. Reaching a fence, swing right past the **lighthouse cottages** and on beside a drive to arrive at the compound gate.

5. First take the path opposite, which

Seaside rock: *The distinctive banded cliffs below St Ann's Head lighthouse*

leads to a viewpoint above a tiny cove where the rock has been dramatically folded. Return to the drive and follow it left past the **old lighthouse**.

Tradition tells of a light on St Ann's Head tended by the priest maintaining a chapel built by Henry Tudor in the 15th century. The first official light, however, was established in the 17th century, although its licence was revoked after the owner levied extortionate dues. In 1714, Trinity House commissioned two lights as transit beacons to guide shipping from the south east past the notorious Crow Rock off Linney Head. The present lighthouse replaced the front light when it was threatened by cliff erosion in 1841. The two lighthouses had separate keepers and staff, who lived in cottages attached to each light. The rear light was deactivated in 1910 and subsequently used by the coastguard. Eventually retired, it was sold as a holiday let, but the front light remains in use and was converted to automatic operation in 1998.

Emerging through the outer gateway, branch off left with the Coast Path to follow the cliffs above **Frenchman's Bay** and **Welshman's Bay**. Beyond **Great**

Castle Head, the site of an Iron Age promontory fort, the path drops to the head of **Westdale Bay**.

6. Turn inland along a shallow valley towards **Dale village**. Through a gate, join a track that runs forward to meet the corner of a lane. Keep ahead, past the **church**. Stick with the main lane to the road. Turn right, back to the car park, to complete the walk. ◆

St Ann's coastguard

The coastguard service was founded in 1822 out of the earlier Preventative Water Guard, which had been established to combat smuggling. Working from a series of watchtowers, coastguards patrolled on both land and sea, and had the additional responsibilities of guarding wrecks to prevent looting. A row of cottages, walled garden and landing on the eastern side of the headland were built to house the station here at St Ann's in 1908.

Thorn Island's fort was built to protect Milford Haven from the French in the1850s

The **Angle peninsula**

*An easy ramble overlooking Milford Haven, passing two
19th-century forts built to resist a French invasion*

What to expect:
*Clear coastal paths
with the return along
a quiet lane*

Distance/time: 6.5 km/ 4 miles. Allow 1½ to 2 hours

Start: Public car park at West Angle Bay

Grid ref: SM 853 031

Ordnance Survey Map: OS Explorer OL36 (South Pembrokeshire)

After the walk: The Old Point House near Angle Point SA71 5AS |
01646 641205, OR the Hibernia Inn, Angle village SA71 5AT | 01646
641517

Walk outline

*Gently climbing above West Angle Bay, the path rounds the
point opposite Thorn Island before turning above sloping cliffs
overlooking the Milford Haven shipping roads. Winding behind
Chapel Fort, the route continues at the edge of coastal woodland
before rounding the eastern point to the tidal shore of Angle Bay.
From Angle village, a quiet lane leads back to the car park.*

Milford Haven

During the 19th century, Milford Haven's naval shipyard
was a potential target for Napoleon's forces and a ring of
elaborate defences was built to counter any invasion. Passed
during the walk are two of the forts, but many of the other
defences strategically sited around the Haven are visible too.
In the event, the French never attacked and developments
in warships and guns soon left the defences obsolete. They
became known as 'Palmerston's Follies' after the Prime Minister
who had ordered their construction.

Pele tower, Angle

Some were reused for coastal defence during the First World
War and again after 1939, when Pembroke Dock was a base for
Sunderland flying boats patrolling the North Atlantic to defend
supply convoys from Nazi U-boats.

Little ringed plover

The Walk

1. Follow a track from the northern end of the car park, passing the ruin of a **lime kiln**. Ignore the path off just beyond and continue a little farther to a bend. Leave there with the **Wales Coast Path**, keeping right to climb onto the promontory overlooking Thorn Island.

2. Rounding the point, the view is along Milford Haven, jetties from oil and gas terminals striding out to provide deepwater berthing. Continue along the coast, shortly angling around the dry-moated defences of **Chapel Bay Fort** to meet the corner of a track by the entrance at the far end.

3. Follow the track ahead past a couple of **cottages**. Where it then splits, keep left through a gate and carry on beside woodland. Beyond the trees, the path continues at the edge of successive fields, eventually dropping to a track down to the **lifeboat station**. Cross

to the ongoing path opposite, which tunnels through scrub before emerging into a meadow. Keep going at the perimeter to the point, where a narrow hedge gap reveals **steps to the shore** and the ruin of the **original Angle lifeboat station**. At low tide you can stick with the stony beach to **The Old Point House**. Otherwise, return to the meadow and follow the edge of fields to the pub.

Passage in and out of Milford Haven has never been easy. Many ships have been driven onto Thorn rocks, the most notable being the SS Loch Shiel, which grounded in January 1894. An iron sailing ship en route to Australia carrying gunpowder, beer and whisky, it had made for Milford Haven seeking shelter from a storm. The Angle lifeboat rescued the captain and 6 crew from the rigging as well as 26 hands and passengers who had escaped onto the rock.

0   1km

½ mile

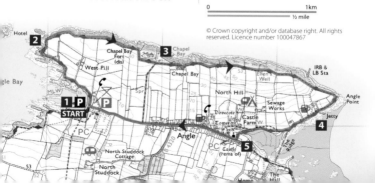

Unhurried inlet: *Boats moored close to Angle village, in Angle Bay*

4. A track leads on above the shore towards the village and may occasionally be briefly flooded at spring tide. Reaching the head of the inlet, branch left over a bridge and keep forward to a junction in **Angle**.

5. Follow the street right through the village, passing **St Andrew's Church**. Although the church is normally closed, wander around the back to see a small **seaman's chapel** dedicated to St Anthony, which was built in 1447 by Edward Shirburn of Nangle. Beyond the village, the lane leads back to the car park at **West Angle**, to complete the walk. ♦

Thorn Island

The fort on Thorn Island was built around 1854 and armed with a battery of nine guns to cover Milford Haven's approach. It complemented the batteries on the Dale peninsula opposite. During the First World War, the fort housed searchlights, but was sold off in 1932 and for a time run as a hotel. Plans to develop it as a luxury resort came to naught and, although sold again, the island's future has yet to be announced.

Looking west from the dunes along Freshwater West beach at half tide

walk 4

Freshwater West & Angle

A longer walk contrasting the rugged southern side of the Angle peninsula with the sheltered shore behind Angle Bay

What to expect:
Rough clifftop paths on the south coast of the peninsula, with a return along quiet lanes

Distance/time: 14.5 km/ 9 miles. Allow 4 to 4½ hourss

Start: Public car park overlooking southern end of Freshwater West

Grid ref: SR 885 998

Ordnance Survey Map: OS Explorer OL36 (South Pembrokeshire)

After the walk: The Hibernia Inn, Angle village SA71 5AT | 01646 641517, OR the Old Point House near Angle Point SA71 5AS | 01646 641205

Walk outline

The walk begins along the broad strand of Freshwater West before climbing onto the undulating cliffs lining the southern flank of the Angle Peninsula, the most demanding part of the day. Rounding Rat Island, the way drops to West Angle Bay, cutting inland along a lane to Angle village. The stretch beside Angle Bay follows a private drive above the shore, the route then turning up through woods over the neck of land and dropping across fields back to the coast.

The Angle peninsula

Directly facing the Atlantic winds, Freshwater West is one of Pembrokeshire's finest surfing beaches, backed by extensive dunes that have blown inland along a shallow valley.

The jagged run of deep-red sandstone cliffs beyond have been battered by those same relentless waves, which in high wind can drive spray over the tops. Among the fascinating rockscapes, look out for Guttle Hole, a natural arch piercing the rock. In contrast, in sheltered Angle Bay the water simply laps against the shore, creeping in and out with the tide to gently rock the flotilla of small boats moored in its shelter.

Surfing at Freshwater West

Otter

The Walk

1. Drop to **Freshwater West beach** and head north, with the sea on your left, along the foot of the dunes. Approaching rocks at the far end, find a path turning inland, which soon swings left to meander atop low cliffs above a succession of small bays. Look back for the changing view of Freshwater West, soon replaced with that ahead across the mouth of Milford Haven to St Ann's Head.

Near the natural arch of **Guttle Hole** is a crumbling octagonal structure, probably an early light or **watchtower**. The path winds on, skirting **Whitedole Bay** to a promontory overlooking **Sheep Island**.

2. Rounding the point, carry on above **Castles Bay**. Shortly, the path turns in above an impressive blowhole in the sandstone cliff, called **Welcome Pit**. The best view is seen as you climb away on the far side of the small valley. Continue to the next point above **Rat Island**.

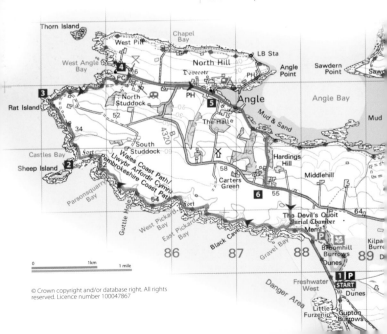

Sheltered water: *The white-painted Old Point House pub seen across Angle Bay*

3. The path runs seaward of a **Victorian gun battery** and past the ruin of a **Tudor blockhouse**.

As early as the 16th century, Milford Haven was a strategic landing and a pair of blockhouses was built to defend the Haven approach. The one on Dale Head has disappeared beneath the Victorian West Blockhouse, but the other one here, is still partially standing. The site was also chosen for a Palmerston fort, but apart from the caretaker's quarters, most of its buildings

have disappeared. The gun emplacements, however, can still be seen to the right of the path.

The path winds through scrub above the coast, the view ahead now to West Angle Bay and Thorn Island. Eventually passing through a gate to break from the scrub, continue at the coastal perimeter of successive fields, losing height and finally turning behind **West Angle beach** to meet the end of a lane by a car park.

4. To make this an even longer ramble, you can follow the instruction in Walk 3

Local industry : *The last of twenty or so seaweed drying huts at Freshwater West*

around the northern coast of the Angle peninsula. Otherwise, take the lane inland and walk through **Angle village**, passing the **Hibernia Inn**.

5. At the far end of the village, where the road swings to the right, keep ahead on a narrow leafy lane. Carry on through a gate as it becomes a private drive, hugging the back of **Angle Bay**. Eventually the drive swings off to the right, leaving the Coast Path. Follow it up through trees towards a gate, but before reaching it, watch for a path branching

off left to meet a gravel track. Turn right, curving up past the gate and climbing to a junction with a lane.

6. Go left for 400 metres to find a path leaving over a stile by a field gate on the right. If you reach the white-towered **Rocket Cart Cottage**, you've gone a little too far.

Built towards the end of the 19th century, Rocket Cart Cottage and lookout tower housed a Board of Trade cliff rescue team. Equipped with a horse cart containing a rope cliff-ladder, rocket-fired rescue line and breaches buoy, the on-call volunteers would race to the assistance of ships foundering off shore. Volunteers were

usually fishermen and seafarers who understood the dangers of violent winds and seas at first-hand.

Walk away at the field edge. Passing into a second field, bear left to a stile at the far side. Drop to a stream at the base of a small valley and turn right towards the coast. Crossing a stile at the bottom, rejoin the **Wales Coast Path** and follow it left, retracing your outward route across **Freshwater West beach** back to the car park to complete the walk. ♦

Laverbread

In the dunes above the beach, the National Park has restored a seaweed drying hut. Until the 1950s, women would follow the tide out in spring to gather purple laver, an edible seaweed. After being washed and dried, it was sent to Swansea to be made into laverbread. Although locally regarded as 'poor man's food', it adds a wonderful flavour to a wide range of dishes and became something of a delicacy for late 19th-century London society.

Elegug Stacks are home to thousands of nesting seabirds in spring and early summer

Elegug Stacks & the Range

The longest walk takes you onto one of the finest and most dramatic sections of the whole Pembrokeshire coast

What to expect:
Rugged clifftop paths, several ups and downs, quiet lanes and long flight of steps

Distance/time: 17.5 km/ 11miles. Allow 4 to 5 hours

Start: Coastal car park above St Govan's Chapel

Grid ref: SR 967 930

Ordnance Survey Map: OS Explorer OL36 (South Pembrokeshire)

After the walk: St Govan's Inn, Bosherston SA71 5DN | 01646 661311

Walk outline

Beginning at the St Govan's Chapel car park lets you stride out during the first part of the day, following the lane back to Bosherston. The route then takes to field paths around the north eastern perimeter of Range East to Merrion Camp before a lane leads back to the coast. After wandering to the Green Bridge, the walk follows the meandering Wales Coast Path above the cliffs all the way back to St Govan's Chapel.

Castlemartin range

Although a challenge because of the walk's length, the cliff path here is no more demanding than some other sections of the coast. However, the walk is likely to occupy the whole day, purely because the constantly changing coastscape and sheer number of superb cliff formations provide so many distractions along the way.

Note: the route lies within an MOD training area, which is in use for around 44 weeks a year — when access is prohibited. However, the walk is generally possible at weekends, during holiday periods and after 16.30. Call 01646 662367 for recorded information.

St Govan's Chapel

Guillemot pair

Huntsman's Leap: *This sea-eroded natural chasm is popular with climbers*

The Walk

1. First walk towards the cliffs, where a stepped path leads to **St Govan's Chapel**, tucked at the bottom of a fissure. Having explored this curious chapel, return to the car park and head back up the lane to **Bosherston**, passing **St Govan's Inn** and into the village. Roughly 400 metres beyond the church, look for a track leaving through a gate on the left.

2. Signed as the '**Castlemartin Range Trail'**, it leads past a disused quarry. Approaching a gate onto **Range East**, turn right to **Carew Farm**, but after 200 metres leave through a gate on the left. Walk forward to a second gate and carry on beside meadows. Nearing a range track, pass through a gate on the right and continue at the perimeter of grazing fields, angling on to meet another track.

Until the late 1930s, the Castlemartin headland was farmed as part of the Stackpole estate, but the area was requisitioned by the Army for armoured

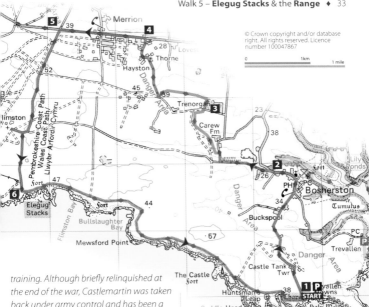

training. Although briefly relinquished at the end of the war, Castlemartin was taken back under army control and has been a major training facility ever since.

3. Cross to the field opposite and walk on at the right edge. Swing left within the corner along the far side and continue beside the hedge in successive fields. Coming out onto a concrete track, go right, immediately forking right again through a gate along a gravel track. Passing the houses and chapel at **Thorne**, it becomes a lane and winds out to the main road.

4. Turn left on a footpath paralleling the road behind a hedge. The hedged

path resumes beyond the entrance to **Merrion Camp**, later running with the edge of a field before passing back onto the road at a crossroads.

5. Warren, with its tall-spired church is to the right, but the onward route is to the left, across the range to the coast. After 1.5 kilometres, the track doglegs near **Flimston Chapel**, which stands over to the right. Continue with the track for another kilometre to a car park behind the cliffs.

Sea arch: *The 'Green Bridge of Wales' is one of the finest natural rock arches in Europe*

Although its origins are obscure, Flimston Chapel is thought to have been connected to the priory at Monkton, already an abbey before the Normans arrived. By the 18th century, it had fallen into secular use and was taken over as a carpenter's workshop. In 1905, the Lambtons of nearby Brownslade restored it as a memorial to their sons killed during the second Boer War. The chapel was again abandoned during the Second World War, but afterwards restored once more, this time by officers and men of the Merrion Camp, and is used for occasional services.

6. First, follow the cliff a short distance to the right to a viewpoint overlooking the **Green Bridge of Wales**, a delicate arch reaching out to an offshore stack that is pounded by the waves below. A wooden platform enables a grand view. Now follow the **Wales Coast Path** east, with the sea on your right, passing the **Elegug Stacks** and the complex formation of caves, coves and blowholes just beyond. Be careful not to stray too close to the dangerous cliff edge.

The path carries on above **Flimston Bay**, past **Moody Nose**, where there is an **Iron Age fort** and then around the back of **Bullslaughter Bay**. Beyond

Mewsford Point, the dramatic sights continue to unfold one after another. The promontory of **The Castle** is another impressive fort, while farther on is a long, narrow cove known as **Huntsman's Leap**. Not far beyond, the path leads back to the car park. And if you didn't do so at the start of the walk, don't forget to have a look at **St Govan's Chapel** before you leave. ♦

A wildlife wonder

For the last 80 years, most of the Castlemartin area has been left largely untouched. Farming ended here before the widespread use of pesticides and fertilisers and the land has since been lightly managed by seasonal grazing. Consequently, the grasslands and dunes are incredibly rich in wildflowers, insects, birds and small mammals, many of them now rare. Prehistoric settlements and burial sites have also survived, giving valuable insights into the past.

Broad Haven beach and dunes with Church Rock just offshore

Bosherston & Broad Haven

A popular walk around the lovely, man-made Lily Ponds to an ancient chapel built into the cliff above a wild shore

What to expect:
Pondside paths, sand, undulating cliff tops, long flight of steps to the chapel

Distance/time: 9 km/ 5½miles. Allow 2½ to 3 hours

Start: Bosherston National Trust car park (pay and display)

Grid ref: SR 967 948

Ordnance Survey Map: OS Explorer OL36 (South Pembrokeshire)

After the walk: St Govan's Inn, Bosherston SA71 5DN | 01646 661311

Walk outline
There is a glimpse of all three arms of the Lily Ponds on the way down to the beach at Broad Haven. Skirting the foot of the dunes, the route climbs onto the cliffs to pick up a path that hugs the coast all the way round St Govan's Head. After climbing down to St Govan's Chapel, you can cut back across the promontory to Broad Haven before returning along the other flank of the Lily Ponds.

Broad Haven and Bosherston
Although the walk incorporates only a short stretch of coast, every twist and turn reveals spectacular scenery. The beach at Broad Haven is superb and the Lily Ponds a pure delight, particularly during summer when the lilies bloom. The location of St Govan's chapel must be one of the most unusual in the country: wedged into a crevice at the base of a sea cliff with the path to the shore passing through it.

Church Rock, Broad Haven

Note: Part of the route lies within a restricted MOD training area. However, the walk is usually possible at weekends, during summer holidays and after 16.30. Call 01646 662367 for information. But even when the range is closed, you can still walk around the Lily Ponds to Broad Haven beach.

Waterlily

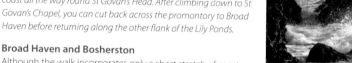

The Walk

1. A path from the bottom of the car park drops to the western arm of the **Lily Ponds**. Keep ahead past a junction to a **causeway** and cross the lake. The path swings right along the northern shore, cresting a rise that gives a fine view along the pools before dropping to a **second causeway**. Over that go right, soon reaching a **third causeway**. Again cross and follow the ongoing path to a junction at the foot of the lakes. Bear left beside the outflow to a **bridge**, cross that and drop left to the **beach**.

Occupying the lower reaches of three wooded valleys that converge behind Broad Haven beach, Bosherston Lily Ponds were created at the end of the 18th century when the outlet stream was dammed. It was part of a grand landscape project undertaken by Sir John Cambell of Cawdor, to whose family the Stackpole estate had passed a century earlier.

They now form part of a vibrant nature reserve, supporting a wide variety of plant and animal life. Butterflies and dragonflies dance in the air, while dabbling on the

0   1km
           ½ mile

water are various waterfowl including moorhen, tufted duck and goosander. If you're lucky you might even see an otter, or lurking beneath the surface, a predatory pike.

Still waters: *Bosherston Lily Ponds in summer*

2. Walk away, curving right at the foot of the dunes. Approaching the far end of **Broad Haven beach**, climb away on a stepped path.

At the top, just before a car park, go left to a gate and on above **Star Rock**. Follow the path above the cliffs (a good place from which to watch surfers in Broad Haven bay) to a **sentry box** at the edge of the range.

3. Assuming the range is open, you can follow the meandering path along the cliff top. Approaching **St Govan's Head**, take a path off to the left, which drops past the head of a narrow inlet. Climb beyond and continue around the promontory. Swing past the **command post** and continue at the edge of **Trevallen Downs** to a junction at **St Govan's** by the car park. A stepped path on the left descends to tiny **St Govan's Chapel** and the boulder beach.

Born in Wexford during the 6th century, Govan became a monk in the monastery at Dairinis. He was eventually elected its Abbot but late in life sailed to

Wave power: *Massive, eroded limestone cliffs and rock stacks near St Govan's Head*

Pembrokeshire, seeking out St David. Approaching land, he was chased by raiders, but managed to reach shore where he hid in a cleft that miraculously opened for him in the cliffs. Unable to find him, the pirates finally left, but Govan decided to stay and became a hermit, ministering to the people who lived nearby.

In the back of the chapel, thought to date from the 11th century, is the cleft in which he is said to have hidden and curious markings on the rock appear to bear the imprint of his spine. One of the many

boulders on the shore supposedly contains a silver bell, hidden there by angels who at Govan's behest retrieved it from the pirates who had stolen it. Legend says that when struck, it will break open to reveal the bell.

4. Climb back to the top of the cliff and turn right, either retracing your outward clifftop route, or taking the more direct main path that cuts across the headland. Continue past the **sentry box** and down to the National Trust's **Broad Haven beach**, walking back to Point **2** by the stream. Cross the bridge off the beach and return to the junction at the foot of the Lily Ponds.

5. Now turn left, re-crossing the outflow to follow a path up the southern shore of the western finger of the ponds. Towards the top of the lake, after passing the ruin of an old **pumphouse**, (which once supplied piped drinking water to the army's nearby Newton Camp) bear off left and climb back to the car park to complete the walk. ♦

St Govan's Chapel

Tiny, atmospheric St Govan's chapel sits at the bottom of a deep cleft in the cliffs, and can be reached only by a long flight of steps. Now a Grade 1 Listed Building cared for by the Pembrokeshire National Park, the limestone chapel certainly existed in Norman times but its origins may date back to the 6th century. Famous visitors have included King Edward VII and Queen Alexandra who declared they were 'delighted with everything they saw'.

Barafundle Bay is regularly voted one of Wales' most beautiful beaches

The **Stackpole Estate**

A wonderfully varied walk taking in a tiny harbour, idyllic beach, stunning clifftop scenery and beautiful lakes

What to expect:
Rugged cliff and dunes paths with occasional ups and downs

Distance/time: 8.5 km/ 5¼ miles. Allow 2 to 2½ hours

Start: Stackpole Quay National Trust car park (pay and display)

Grid ref: SR 991 958

Ordnance Survey Map: OS Explorer OL36 (South Pembrokeshire)

After the walk: The Stackpole Inn, Stackpole SA71 5DF | 01646 672324, OR the National Trust's Boathouse Tearoom (seasonal), Stackpole Quay SA71 5LS | 01646 672687

Walk outline

After exploring Stackpole's tiny harbour, the walk follows the cliffs to secluded Barafundle Bay. Continuing around Stackpole Head, the scenery becomes increasingly dramatic, with a succession of natural arches, stacks and blowholes. At Broad Haven, there is a short stretch beside dunes before tracing the banks of the Bosherston Lily Ponds and returning to the coast across the fields.

Barafundle Bay and Stackpole Head

Barafundle Bay is acknowledged as the finest in Wales, due in part, perhaps, to the fact that it can only be reached by a ¼ hour walk. Go there mid-week out of season and you're likely to have the place to yourself.

Barafundle steps

The rest of the coast is equally stunning, particularly on the western side of Stackpole Head, where the sheer limestone cliffs are exposed to the full fury of Atlantic gales. Caves pierce Stackpole Head, while beyond is a succession of rocky bays, ragged points and crumbling stacks, all footed by bouldery debris endlessly battered by the waves. In spring, the cliffs are colonised by breeding seabirds, every conceivable ledge serving as a noisy nesting place.

Chough

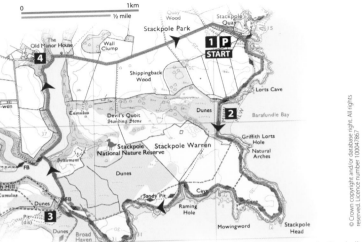

The Walk

1. Head back towards the National Trust's **Boathouse Tearoom**, passing behind it on a path signed to 'Barafundle'.

The Stackpole estate has a long history. Viking adventurers left their stamp in the very name 'Stac Pollr', a rock marking an inlet, which admirably describes Church Rock opposite Broad Haven. The earliest known building was a Norman castle built by Elidur de Stackpole in the 11th century. The estate passed through the generations by descent or marriage, being sold only once in the 17th century to the Lorts.

It then passed by marriage to the Cambells of Cawdor in Scotland, who replaced the castle with a Palladian mansion, which overlooked the head of the eastern valley. They also began landscaping the park, planting more than 1,000 trees, many of which were exotic species provided by Sir Joseph Banks, the founder of Kew Gardens.

A first attempt to create a lake below the house was unsuccessful as the water drained away through the limestone, but in 1860 a small dam below the confluence of the valleys solved the problem, creating the famous Lily Ponds.

The onward route is up steps to the right, but first walk a short distance

Exposed coast: *Stackpole Quay is protected by massive stone breakwaters*

forward to see the small harbour at **Stackpole Quay**.

The Cambells were keen sailors and moored their yacht Speedwitch in the small harbour. The quay was built in the 18th century around the time of the new house and used to export limestone dug from a small quarry behind the lime kiln that stands at the head of the beach.

It also served as a landing for supplies to Stackpole Court such as coal. Heating the large house required great quantities and it was much more readily transported by boat than horse and cart along narrow, unsurfaced lanes.

At the top of the steps, the path ahead gives another view to the quay; otherwise turn through an arch and continue onto a **grassy headland**.

A clear path cuts across the headland, but lesser paths trace the ins and outs of the cliffs. However, be careful, for the drops are sheer and the edge sometimes unstable.

Beautiful beach: *Steps lead down to Barafundle Bay on the Stackpole estate*

Rounding the headland, paths converge to another **stone archway** above **Barafundle Bay**. Curving steps lead down to the beach.

2. Cross the beach below the **dunes** to the far side, where a stepped path climbs through a grove of sycamores, regaining the cliff top through a kissing gate.

Again, you can cut across the headland, but the interest lies in the dramatic clifftop scenery as you round the point of **Stackpole Head** and trace the meandering rim of its western edge. The path passes several **blowholes** at different stages of evolution; ultimately they will all become coves open to the sea.

Rounding **Saddle Point**, the path turns in above **Broad Haven** to a final gate at the edge of the dunes. If the tide is out, drop down to the beach and walk into the narrowing cove to find a **footbridge** at the head of a small pool. Otherwise, keep ahead through the dunes beside a buried **estate wall**, descending beyond to a path at the foot of the ponds.

3. Cross the **stream** and then bear right beside a **second bridge** to join the path

coming in from the dunes. The way ahead is signed to 'Bosherston'. To the left, there are glimpses of the lower lake before passing into trees. Over a **causeway** spanning the northern arm of the pools, turn right above the shore.

4. Reaching an **arched bridge**, cross to the east bank. Pass through a gate and follow a track away between the fields. Keep ahead past junctions, eventually emerging through a gate into the car park to complete the walk. ◆

Stackpole Court

Stackpole Court was home to the Barons and Earls of Cawdor for almost 200 years. Amongst those entertained at the house were Lord Nelson and Sir William and Lady Hamilton. But the the loss of 6,000 acres to the Army at Castlemartin compromised the economics of the estate. The house slowly deteriorated and was demolished in 1963. On the death of the 5th Earl in 1970, the estate was broken up and the coastal park given to the National Trust.

Manorbier Castle seen from the Wales Coast Path near Priest's Nose

Manorbier

Overlooking a sunny bay, Manorbier and its medieval castle are treasured gems on the Pembrokeshire coast

What to expect:
Good coastal paths with several ups and downs, quiet lanes

Distance/time: 8 km/5 miles. Allow 2 to 2½ hours

Start: Manorbier beach car park (pay and display)

Grid ref: SS 063 976

Ordnance Survey Map: OS xplorer OL36 (South Pembrokeshire)

After the walk: Castle Inn, Manorbier SA70 7TE | 01834 871268, OR Beach Break Tearooms in Manorbier village SA70 7TD | 01834 871709

Walk outline

After detouring to the delightful church of St James, the walk follows a narrow lane out of the village and across fields to the coast. Swinging back above impressive sandstone cliffs, the way winds around Priest's Nose, crossing Manorbier beach to continue above its western cliffs to the secluded Swanlake Bay. The unhurried return is along field paths and lane.

Manorbier and its coast

Manorbier Castle is the birthplace of Gerald of Wales, who, although widely travelled, always referred to Manorbier as the best place in all of Wales. Sheltering in a gentle valley and footed by a fine beach that looks out past St Govan's, it is an enchanting spot that could entice you to while away the day.

However, you would then miss out on the stunning cliffscapes on either side of the bay. Layers of richly coloured sandstone, tilted upright face-on to the sea, have created an intriguing coastline. Sheer cliffs are broken into isolated stacks and incised by narrow slots constantly washed by the waves. Near the top of Priest's Nose is a Neolithic burial chamber, while Swanlake Bay has a wonderful and usually deserted beach.

King's Quoit dolmen

Ox-eye daisies

The Walk

1. A path from the car park below **Manorbier Castle** (fee payable) leads up to nearby **St James' Church**.

Initially a simple timber motte and bailey, the castle was founded by Odo de Barri soon after the Norman conquest. It was rebuilt in stone by his son William and remained in de Barri hands until the 14th century. Although impressively equipped, the castle served largely as a fortified manor house. However, it was taken during the Civil War by the Parliamentarians and slighted, the damage beginning a long period of decay. The castle was restored in the 19th century.

Having looked around the church, follow the lane back down to the **village** and turn right. Keep right past a junction and then go right again beside **Castlemead**. At a fork, branch left and continue past a cottage to cross a stile beside a gate at the end.

2. Over another stile on the right, head away across the fields up to a stile at **Hill Farm**. Walk on, passing a barn on your right. Reaching a gate in the right wall, turn through. Cross the next field and swing left beside the wall down to join the **Wales Coast Path**.

3. Follow it right through a gate above an impressive section of the coast, the upended strata of sandstone cut back in a succession of tiny coves. Before the path rounds **Priest's Nose** the view ahead is to Trewent Point and Stackpole. Carry on past the head of a couple of dramatic chasms incised into the cliff, beyond which is a Neolithic burial chamber, the **King's Quoit**. The ongoing path drops to **Manorbier beach**.

4. Walk across the head of the beach and over a stream at the far side. Climb away with the ongoing Coast Path below the road. After a lay-by, bear left on a drive down to a cottage. Through a

Gull's-eye view: *Manorbier Castle and St James' Church from the air*

gate, carry on above the rocks. Beyond a shallow cove, the path swings up a ridge of upturned strata. At the end, turn in above **Swanlake Bay**, dropping towards the back of the beach.

5. Through a gate, fork right and zigzag uphill. Continue climbing at the edge of a field, turning right through a kissing gate near the top to **East Moor Farm**. Bear right past farm buildings to another kissing gate. Cross a track and keep ahead beside a high hedge, finally emerging onto a lane. Follow it right towards **Manorbier**, passing above the beach back to the car park to complete the walk. ♦

St James' Church

Dedicated to St James the Greater, Apostle and Martyr, the church stands slightly apart from the village and overlooks the valley opposite the castle. Contemporary with the castle, it occupies the site of a 6th-century Celtic monastery founded by St Pyr, from whose name Manorbier derived, 'belonging to Pyr'. The unusual, tall, castellated tower perhaps served as a lookout across the bay to complement that on the castle.

Pastel-hued houses in Tenby's 'Old Town' reflected in the tranquil harbour

Tenby & Giltar Point

A fine walk around Tenby, featuring superb beaches and clifftop views overlooking the monastic island of Caldy

What to expect:
Town streets, beach, dunes and a good path along the cliff

Distance/time: 10km/ 6¼ miles. Allow 2½ to 3 hours

Start: South Beach car park (pay and display)

Grid ref: SN 130 000

Ordnance Survey Map: OS Explorer OL36 (South Pembrokeshire)

After the walk: Wide choice of pubs and cafés in Tenby

Walk outline

A stroll around the old town, harbour and castle hill is a prelude to striding out along the beach to Giltar Point. After an impressive stretch along the cliffs, the walk turns down to the small village of Penally and then back through the dunes and across the sands to Tenby.

Tenby

Settled by the Vikings, Tenby evolved as a fishing and trading port and had a fortress to defend its trade by the time the Normans arrived. Despite uprisings by the Welsh, the town's affluence grew throughout the medieval period, from which time the harbour, town walls and several sturdy houses survive.

Tudor Merchant's House

Tenby's prosperity ended with the Civil War when the town was attacked by both sides and then sacked after a three-day siege by the Parliamentarians. Soon afterwards, the town was decimated when the plague hit in 1648. The town never recovered and 150 years later, John Wesley recorded that pigs roamed among abandoned houses. It was not until the 18th century that the town revived. Although little now remains of the castle, the nearby museum tells more of Tenby's story.

Rock pipit

The Walk

1. Leave the bottom end of the car park and follow the **Esplanade** above the beach. Swing left along **St Florence Parade** and turn beneath the **Five Arch Gate** into the **old town**.

Tenby developed as a resort at the beginning of the 19th century, at a time when High Society's continental travel was curtailed by the Napoleonic wars. Financed by William Paxton, who had made his fortune as Master of the Mint in Bengal and a financial trader back in England, the town quickly became fashionable as a seaside spa, its success consolidated half a century later when the railway arrived in 1863. Tenby avoided many of the crass developments that often accompany seaside

popularity and it remains an attractive place, the town walls, old streets and a picturesque harbour all contributing to its appeal.

At the end of **St George's Street**, bear left to a junction behind **St Mary's Church** and walk right along **St Julian's Street**. After 100 metres, turn left past the **Lifeboat Tavern** into a narrow passage. Keep ahead beyond the

National Trust's **Tudor Merchant's House** to emerge on **Crackwell Street**. Go right in to **Castle Square**.

Built around the end of the 15th century, the Tudor Merchant's House is one of the oldest surviving houses in the town and was owned

Holiday heaven?: *Tenby Old Town, the harbour and St Catherine's Island from the air*

by a prosperous merchant who lived 'over the shop'. Tenby traded with the world and exotic imports such as wine, spices, olive oil and fine fabrics would have appeared beside locally produced woollen cloth, pottery and coal. Archaeological investigation (notably of the cesspit below the indoor latrine) has revealed that the family lived well and the house has been furnished and brightly decorated to illustrate in a very hands-on way what the family's life might have been like.

2. First, turn sharp left past the **Seamen's Rooms** to have a look at the **harbour** and **North Beach**. Return to Castle Square and bear left, passing **Laxton House** to round **Castle Hill**, where the former and present **lifeboat stations** stand side by side. The path returns you to Point **2**.

If the tide is out, you can turn sharp left through an **archway to South Beach** and follow the base of the cliffs below the town. Otherwise, you'll have to walk through the town. In which case, bear left along **St Julian's Street**

Summer dusk: *Tenby Old Town, harbour and lifeboat station on a summer's night*

to the **Buccaneer Inn**, there going left along **Cob Lane**. Emerging onto **Cresswell Street**, go left and then right at the bottom, continuing along the **Esplanade** and eventually down to the beach.

3. Walk away below the dunes towards the cliffs at the far end of **South Beach** beneath **Giltar Point**, where a stepped path climbs onto the headland. Through a gate at the top, continue above old quarries and around the tip of Giltar Point. Another gate takes you onto the

MOD firing range. Keep going through a couple more gates to another at the far side of the range.

4. Do not pass through, instead turn right and head down beside a fence. At the bottom, go through a gate on the left and walk beneath the railway out to the main road. Follow it right. Just before **Penally Station** car park, turn left into the **village** and then go right to have a look at the **church**.

5. Return to the lane below the church. Through a waymarked gate, a track drops through **Penally Court Farm** to the main road. Cross to the **Wales**

Coast Path, which leaves along a track opposite, beside Penally Station car park. Carefully cross the **railway line** and follow the path across the **firing range** and on to the edge of a **golf course**. The path winds across the fairway and dunes to the beach. Turn left towards Tenby, leaving the beach at the far end of the dunes back to the car park to complete the walk. ♦

St Catherine's Island

A tiny chapel gave the island its name before it was commandeered as a fort, part of the 19th-century defences against Napoleon's navy. The fort eventually became a private house but was requisitioned in the Second World War as an anti-aircraft battery. During the 1970s it became a zoo, but after lying empty for many years, has now been restored and is open at weekends.

The summerhouse at the National Trust's Colby Woodland Garden

Colby Woodland Garden

Beach, cliffs, woods and walled garden combine in a lovely walk at the southern end of the Pembrokeshire Coast Path

What to expect:
Good paths and tracks with minimal road walking, some ups and downs

Distance/time: 8km/ 5 miles. Allow 2 to 2½ hours

Start: Car park in Amroth, off Brookside Villas, behind the Amroth Arms

Grid ref: SN 162 070

Ordnance Survey Map: OS Explorer OL36 (South Pembrokeshire)

After the walk: Bothy tearoom at Colby Woodland Garden SA67 8PP | 01834 811885, OR the Amroth Arms in Amroth SA67 8NG | 01834 812480

Walk outline

After a brief stroll along the front, and climbing onto the cliffs for the view, the route wanders through woodland into the higher reaches of the Colby valley. Climbing over an open hill the way drops through a tributary valley to Colby, where you can break the walk to explore the walled garden. A broad track then heads back down the valley to Amroth.

The Colby valley

Although hardly apparent today, the Colby valley was once the heart of a thriving mining industry, the prize being rich seams of anthracite, the most valued of all coals. Both coal and iron ore had been mined in the area throughout the medieval period, but it was the industrial age that suddenly created an insatiable demand.

John Colby began operations here at the end of the 18th century and, hidden in the surrounding woods, are many old adits and relics of the industry. Out of the profits, he built Colby Lodge, which was later bought by Samuel Kay, a pharmacist from Stockport, who began the garden. It passed to the National Trust in 1979.

Amroth village

Peacock butterfly

0   1km
½ mile

The Walk

1. Walk to the sea front by the **Amroth Arms** and go right. As the road turns from the coast, leave beside toilets and climb onto the **headland**. Continue along a narrow meadow, from which there is a grand view across the bay. Partway along, turn out through a gate on the right and follow a hedged path right back down to the lane.

2. Go left for 30 metres before leaving along a private road on the right. Beyond cottages, the way runs as a path along the wooded valley side, later losing height to a junction. Pass through the gate ahead and, ignoring side paths, climb gently through the **Colby valley**, where there are views to the **lodge** and **walled garden**. Emerging through a gate at the far end, drop right, crossing a bridge beside a ford to reach a lane.

Colby sits on the edge of the rich South Wales coal field, and although the quality was still high, the seams were very shallow, sometimes barely 18 inches deep. Long adits followed the seams into the hillside, with children often being used to drag loaded tubs out along the constricted tunnels. Ingressing water was an ever-constant problem and John

Focal point: *A box hedge-lined 'rill' leads up to Colby's distinctive summerhouse*

Colby, in collaboration with his neighbour who worked the seams in the adjacent valley, dug a long drainage sough beneath the workings to take the water out to the beach. Although a profitable enterprise while it lasted, the reserves were worked out within 30 years and the valley quickly reverted to its natural woodland state.

3. Walk left for 250 metres. Just before a bridge, bear right beside a drive on a bridleway marked as the '**Knight's Way**'.

It rises along the upper valley, later taking a higher line above the stream and ultimately climbing to a gate.

4. Turn immediately right to a higher track and follow that to the right, back along the top of the valley. At its end, cross a stile beside a gate on the left and head away by the lefthand hedge. Continue in the next field, bending right within the corner. At the next corner, mount a stile on the left and bear across to a gap in the bottom boundary. Follow the hedge left to a stile in the bottom corner.

Sand and sea: *Long timber groynes protect Amroth's broad, sandy beach*

5. Down a few steps, the path swings right along the top edge of a wood. Shortly climbing another stile, follow a broader path left. Keep with it as it later winds back to the right. Approaching the bottom, the bridlepath veers off to the left across the base of the valley. However, instead go right past a barrier on a narrower path, which runs above a wooded marsh, originally a reservoir whose water powered machinery in the pits lower down the valley. Continue down the valley to emerge onto a lane.

Go left and the turn right into **Colby Woodland Garden**.

Samuel Kay bought the estate in 1873. He began the work of setting out the garden, an undertaking continued by his descendant and then by Peter and Pamela Chance, who bought Colby Lodge in 1965. The Chances commissioned the American artist Lincoln Tabor to paint the marvellous trompe l'oeil in the gazebo at the top of the walled garden. They gave the woodland gardens to the National Trust and the lodge was taken over by Anthony and Cynthia Scourfield-Lewis, who continued to work on the walled garden before giving that to the Trust in 2010.

6. Walk past the entrance to the **walled garden, toilets and tearoom** (For opening times, tickets and events, see the National Trust website: www.nationaltrust.org.uk/colby-woodland-garden) and stay with the track ahead through the woods. Eventually coming out onto a street at the foot of the valley, keep going towards the coast where you will find the car park off on the right, to complete the walk. ♦

Fossilised tree stumps

Ice covered much of Wales during the last Ice Age. Sea levels were 40 metres lower than they are today, and Caldey Island was a small hill overlooking a tundra plain that is now Carmarthen Bay. But as the ice 'retreated', global sea levels rose rapidly. Today, low tides reveal a 'submerged forest' at Amroth. The preserved stumps of willow, hazel, pine, oak and birch are a timely reminder of the dramatic effects of climate change.

Useful Information

Wales Coast Path
Comprehensive information on all sections of the Wales Coast Path can be found at: www.walescoastpath.gov.uk

Visit Pembrokeshire
Pembrokeshire's official tourism website covers everything from accommodation and special events to attractions and adventure. www.visitpembrokeshire.com

Pembrokeshire Coast National Park
The Pembrokeshire Coast National Park website also has information on things to see and do, plus a host of practical details to help plan your visit: www.pembrokeshirecoast.org.uk

Tourist Information Centres
The main TICs provide free information on everything from accommodation and travel to what's on and walking advice.

St David's	01437 720392 | info@orielyparc.co.uk
Milford Haven	01437 771818 | milford.tic@pembrokeshire.gov.uk
Pembroke	01437 776499 | pembroke.tic@pembrokeshire.gov.uk
Tenby	01834 845040 | tenbycentre@pembrokeshirecoast.org.uk
Tenby	01437 775603 | tenby.tic@pembrokeshire.gov.uk
Saundersfoot	01834 813672 | saundersfoot.tic@pembrokeshire.gov.uk

Travel
Main **railway stations** are located at Tenby, Pembroke and Pembroke Dock. Information is available from National Rail Enquiries on 08457 484950 or **www. nationalrail.com.uk**. A dedicated **bus network** serves the whole of the Coast Path, running every day during the summer months but with a limited service in winter. Pembrokeshire Greenways – 01437 776313 – www.pembrokeshiregreenways.co.uk/ Traveline Cymru – 0871 200 22 33 – www.travelinecymru.info

Weather
The Met Office operates a 24 hour online weather forecast for the Ceredigion coastline. See **www.metoffice.gov.uk**